Pressure Co

Pressure Cooker Box Set

Crock Pot Recipes & Pressure Cooker Cookbook

Table Of Contents

Introduction

First book contains 40+ delicious and satisfying Crock Pot recipes that the whole family is sure to enjoy. Each recipe calls for simple and easy to find ingredients, and beginner to intermediate level cooking skills.

Start your day bright eyed and bushy tailed by preparing slow cooked breakfast dishes such as the broccoli and bacon quiche and peanut butter and jelly oatmeal that you can whip up the night before.

Warm up your tummies with savory soups, stews, chowders, and chilis, such as the classic chicken soup and the bacon and corn chowder.

For lunches and dinners, you no longer have to spend so much time in the kitchen. All you need to do is throw together the ingredients for your main course. Choose from a variety of slow cooked beef, lamb, pork, poultry and seafood dishes.

Of course, everyone in the family needs to have their everyday serving of vegetables. Stir together a medley of vegetables in your Crock Pot that even the kids will love!

Last but not the least, dig your forks into Crock Pot desserts apple bread pudding and carrot cake. Who says you cannot slow cook your sweets?

In addition second book contains simple and easy to prepare recipes cooked using a pressure cooker that the whole family will enjoy.

Pressure-cooked food has a lot of health benefits. For one, the nutrients and flavor of the food are retained. In addition, it is deemed as one of the most energy-efficient methods of cooking. This is because pressure cooking cuts the time required to cook using conventional methods by as much as 70%.

This is ideal for working people who need to rush home from work to prepare freshly cooked meals for the family. What's more, after the dish is done, clean up is a breeze. After all, there is only one pot to clean.

Aside from the recipes, you will also learn various tips on how to get the best results when cooking meals using the pressure cooker. Once you learn the basics, you are ready to experiment and whip up your own recipes based on your particular taste and preferences.

Let's begin the journey.

Crock Pot Recipes

Chapter 1: Breakfast

No Crust Broccoli and Bacon Quiche

Number of Servings: 4

You'll Need:

- 1 1/2 cups frozen broccoli florets, thawed
- 1 1/2 cups grated cheese (cheddar, Monterrey Jack, vegan)
- 3 large eggs
- 4 slices cooked bacon
- 1 1/2 cups whole milk (dairy or nut-based)
- 1/3 tsp Dijon mustard
- 3/4 Tbsp mayonnaise
- Water
- Sea salt
- Freshly ground black pepper
- Nonstick cooking spray

How to Prepare:

1. Lightly grease a casserole dish using the nonstick cooking spray. Arrange the broccoli in a single layer on the dish. Spread the cheese on top, then arrange the bacon on top of the cheese.

2. Crack open the eggs into a bowl and whisk. Beat in the milk, mustard, mayonnaise, and a dash of salt and pepper. Pour the mixture on top of the layer of bacon.

3. Place the cooking rack into the Crock Pot. Put the casserole dish on the rack. Pour just enough water into the Crock Pot to submerge the lower half of the casserole dish.

4. Cover and cook for 4 hours on low. Remove the cover and take out the casserole dish. Slice and serve.

Chocolate Chip Pumpkin Bread

Number of Servings: 8

You'll Need:

- 1 cup pumpkin, solid packed
- 1/2 cup coconut or light brown sugar
- 2 Tbsp coconut oil
- 1/4 cup maple syrup
- 1 tsp pure vanilla extract
- 2 tsp baking powder
- 1 3/4 cups all purpose flour, unbleached
- 1/2 tsp ground cinnamon
- 1/2 tsp ground allspice
- 1/2 tsp ground nutmeg
- 1/2 tsp salt
- 1/2 cup chocolate chips, semi sweet
- Nonstick cooking spray

How to Prepare:

1. Grease the Crock Pot with nonstick cooking spray.
2. Mix together the pumpkin, maple syrup, sugar, vanilla extract, and coconut oil in a bowl.

3. In another bowl, mix together the salt, baking powder, flour, nutmeg, allspice, and cinnamon. Pour the flour mixture gradually into the pumpkin mixture as you stir; do not over-mix.

4. Fold the chocolate chips into the batter until evenly distributed, then pour into the Crock Pot.

5. Place a clean towel over the Crock Pot to cover, then place the lid on top. Cook for 2 hours on high or for 5 hours on low, or until bread becomes firm. Turn off the heat and let it stand for 10 minutes before you slice.

Cinnamon Apple Risotto

Number of Servings: 4

You'll Need:

- 2 1/2 Tbsp melted butter
- 1 cup Arborio rice
- 3/4 cup apple juice
- 2 cups milk
- 2 small apples, peeled, cored, sliced thinly
- 1/4 cup brown sugar or coconut sugar
- 1 tsp ground cinnamon
- Freshly ground nutmeg
- Ground cloves

How to Prepare:

1. Pour the melted butter into the Crock Pot and swirl in the rice to coat.

2. Pour in the apple juice and milk. Carefully stir in the apples, sugar, and cinnamon. Add a dash of ground nutmeg and cloves and stir to combine.

3. Cover and cook for 8 hours on low, or until rice is creamy and fluffy. Best served with dried fruit, such as raisins, and milk.

Peanut Butter and Jelly Oatmeal

Number of Servings: 8

You'll Need:

- 2 cups oats, steel cut
- 6 1/2 cups filtered water
- 1 tsp salt
- 1 1/2 tsp ground cinnamon
- 3/4 cup jam of choice (strawberry, blueberry, guava, etc)
- 3/4 cup creamy peanut butter, room temperature
- Unsweetened almond milk
- Nonstick cooking spray

How to Prepare:

1. Grease the Crock Pot with nonstick cooking spray.
2. Mix together the water, oats, cinnamon, and salt in it. Cover and cook for 8 hours on low.
3. Stir the peanut butter into the oatmeal until thoroughly incorporated, then stir in the jam. Serve warm with almond milk.

Walnut and Banana Frittata

Number of Servings: 4

You'll Need:

- 3/4 Tbsp butter
- 2 small ripe bananas
- 8 cups cubed bread
- 6 oz cream cheese
- 3/4 cup chopped walnuts
- 8 large eggs
- 1/6 cup maple syrup
- 3/4 cup heavy cream or whole milk
- 1/6 tsp salt

How to Prepare:

1. About 12 hours before cooking time, grease the inside of the Crock Pot using the butter. Arrange 4 cups of the cubed bread in the bottom.

2. Cube the cream cheese and spread half on top of the cubed bread. Dice1 ripe banana and arrange on top of the cream cheese. Top with half of the chopped walnuts. Repeat the layer with the remaining cubed bread, banana, cream cheese, and walnuts.

3. In a bowl, whisk the eggs until frothy, then beat in the cream or milk, maple syrup, and the salt. Pour the mixture into the Crock Pot. Cover and chill for 12 hours.

4. Take the Crock out of the fridge and attach it to its heat source. Cover and cook for 6 hours on low. Best served with warmed maple syrup.

Chapter 2: Soups

Mushroom and Barley Soup

Number of Servings: 6

You'll Need:

- 3/4 cup boiling water
- 3/4 oz dried porcini mushrooms
- 1 tsp butter or margarine
- 3 oz sliced fresh shiitake mushrooms
- 3 oz sliced fresh button mushrooms
- 1 small onion, diced
- 1 small clove garlic, minced
- 1/3 cup medium pearl barley
- 1/6 tsp freshly ground black pepper
- 1/3 tsp sea salt
- 4 cups vegetable stock

How to Prepare:

1. Place the dried porcini mushrooms in a heat-resistant bowl and pour in the boiling water. Set aside for 12 minutes or more to soak.

2. Place a skillet over medium flame and add the butter or margarine. Once melted, stir in the fresh shiitake and button mushrooms, onion, and garlic. Sauté until onion becomes translucent. Scrape into the Crock Pot.

3. Drain the porcini mushrooms; throw away the soaking water. Add the mushrooms into the Crock Pot.

4. Add the barley into the Crock Pot together with the pepper, salt, and vegetable stock. Stir to distribute the ingredients evenly. Cover and cook on low for 6 hours.

Classic Chicken Soup

Number of Servings: 6

You'll Need:

- 2 1/2 lb chicken pieces, rinsed
- 3 cups chicken stock
- 1 tsp sea salt
- 1/3 tsp freshly ground black pepper
- 1/3 tsp dried thyme
- 1/3 tsp dried basil
- 1 bay leaf
- 1 large onion, chopped
- 1 large carrot, sliced
- 1 1/2 celery stalks, sliced
- 1 large clove garlic
- 2/3 cup chopped parsley
- 1 1/2 cups water
- 3/4 cup frozen corn, thawed
- 3/4 cup frozen peas, thawed
- 5 oz canned mushrooms, drained and chopped
- 4 oz flat noodles

How to Prepare:

1. Combine the chicken pieces, onion, carrot, celery, garlic, parsley, chicken stock, salt, pepper, basil, thyme, and bay leaf in the Crock Pot.

2. Add the water and stir to combine. Cover and cook for 8 hours on low.

3. Take out the cooked chicken parts and set aside to cool to room temperature, then shred by hand; save the bones and skin for making stock, otherwise, discard.

4. Return the chicken into the Crock Pot and stir in the peas, corn, noodles, and mushrooms. Cover and cook for 30 minutes on high.

5. Adjust seasonings to taste, if needed. Take out the bay leaf, then serve.

Chickpea Soup

Number of Servings: 4

You'll Need:

- 1 small onion, diced
- 1 clove garlic, minced
- 20 oz canned chickpeas, drained and rinsed
- 3 cups vegetable broth
- 1 Tbsp freshly squeezed lemon juice
- 1/3 tsp cumin
- 2/3 tsp salt
- 3/4 Tbsp olive oil
- 1/6 tsp chopped fresh parsley

How to Prepare:

1. Combine the onion, garlic, chickpeas, and vegetable broth in the Crock Pot. Add the cumin and salt.

2. Cover and cook for 4 hours on low. Turn off the heat and let cool to room temperature. Puree the soup with an immersion blender or with a food processor or blender.

3. With the soup back in the Crock Pot, stir in the olive oil, parsley, and lemon juice. Cook for half an hour on low. Serve warm.

Tortellini Soup

Number of Servings: 8

You'll Need:

- 18 oz canned diced tomatoes
- 2 cups chicken broth
- 2/3 tsp crushed dried basil
- 1/3 tsp freshly ground black pepper
- 2 cups water
- 1 cup sliced carrots
- 1 cup broccoli florets
- 1 cup spinach
- 1 cup frozen peas
- 10 oz mushrooms, chopped
- 12 oz refrigerated tortellini
- Chopped fresh parsley
- Shaved Parmesan cheese

How to Prepare:

1. Combine the tomatoes, chicken broth, basil, and black pepper in the Crock Pot.

2. Pour in the water, and stir in the carrots, broccoli, spinach, and peas. Cover and cook for 3 hours on high.

3. Stir in the peas, tortellini, and mushrooms. Cover and cook for an additional 1 hour on high, or until the tortellini becomes tender.

4. Ladle into soup bowls and top with fresh parsley and Parmesan cheese. Serve warm.

Orzo and Spinach Soup

Number of Servings: 4

You'll Need:

- 2 Tbsp lemon juice
- 1 clove garlic, minced
- 3/4 tsp lemon zest
- 1 small onion, sliced very thinly
- 4 cups chicken broth
- 3 cups fresh baby spinach
- 3/4 cup cooked cubed chicken breast
- 1/4 cup dried orzo

How to Prepare:

1. Combine the broth, lemon juice and zest, onion, and garlic in the Crock Pot. Cover and cook for 6 hours on low.

2. Add the cooked cubed chicken breast, cover, and cook for half an hour on high. Stir in the spinach and orzo. Cover and cook for an extra 15 minutes. Stir well, then ladle into soup bowls and serve.

Chapter 3: Stews

Simple Irish Coddle

Number of Servings: 8

You'll Need:

- 8 bacon slices, sliced into bite sized pieces
- 2 lb pork sausage
- 1 1/2 large yellow onions, peeled and minced
- 4 large potatoes, peeled and cubed
- 4 large carrots, peeled and cubed
- 1 1/2 cups chicken broth or water or beer or hard cider
- Sea salt
- Freshly ground black pepper

How to Prepare:

1. Place a large skillet over medium high flame and sauté the sausage and bacon pieces together until browned. Break up the sausage, then add the onion and season with salt and pepper. Sauté until onion becomes translucent.

2. Transfer the mixture into a heat proof colander to drain the fat; throw away the excess fat. Pour half of the meat mixture into the Crock Pot and add the cubed potatoes on top, followed by the cubed carrot.

3. Pour the remaining meat mixture on top, then add the liquid. Cover and cook for 6 hours on low.

4. Stir well and adjust seasoning to taste, if needed. Ladle the stew into bowls and serve warm.

Classic Beef Stew

Number of Servings: 8

You'll Need:

- 2 lb lean stew beef, sliced into bite sized chunks
- 3 cups chopped carrots
- 3 cups chopped potatoes
- 1 cup sliced red and/or green bell pepper
- 1 1/2 tsp mixed steak seasoning
- 16 oz canned condensed tomato soup
- 1 cup beef broth
- 2 bay leaves
- 12 oz canned mushrooms, drained
- Sea salt
- Freshly ground black pepper

How to Prepare:

1. Place the chopped potatoes and carrots in the Crock Pot. Place the beef on top and sprinkle the mixed steak seasoning all over.

2. Combine the tomato soup and broth in a bowl, then pour into the Crock Pot. Mix in the bay leaf.

3. Cover and cook for 9 hours on low. Stir in the mushrooms, cover, and cook for an additional 1 hour.

4. Remove the bay leaf, adjust seasoning to taste with salt and pepper, if needed, and serve.

Thyme Tilapia Stew

Number of Servings: 8

You'll Need:

- 6 Tbsp butter
- 3 lb frozen boneless tilapia fillets
- 21 oz canned diced tomatoes with juices
- 2/3 cup sliced green onion
- 6 cloves garlic, minced
- 3 tsp Thai fish sauce
- 3 Tbsp chopped fresh thyme or 1 1/2 tsp dried thyme
- Nonstick cooking spray

How to Prepare:

1. Coat the Crock Pot with nonstick cooking spray, then add the butter, tilapia, tomatoes with their juices, garlic, and green onion. Sprinkle the fish sauce and thyme all over and carefully stir to combine.

2. Cover and cook for 2 hours on high or for 3 hours on low, or less depending on how thick the fillets are.

3. To check if fillets are cooked through, flake with a fork. Break up the fillets and mix it well. Best served with pasta or rice.

Vegetable Lover's Stew

Number of Servings: 6

You'll Need:

- 2 small zucchini, unpeeled, sliced thickly
- 1 large carrot, sliced thickly
- 2 tomatoes, seeded and chopped
- 1 small red onion, chopped
- 3/4 cup sliced celery
- 10 oz canned chickpeas, rinsed and drained
- 10 oz canned black beans, rinsed and drained
- 2 cups vegetable stock
- 4 oz canned tomato paste
- 3/4 tsp crushed dried basil
- 3/4 tsp crushed dried oregano
- 1/3 tsp sea salt
- 1/6 tsp freshly ground black pepper
- 1/6 tsp red pepper flakes
- 3 cloves garlic
- 1 bay leaf
- 1/3 cup pitted black olives, halved
- Minced fresh parsley

- Lime wedges

How to Prepare:

1. Place the carrots, zucchini, tomatoes, onion, celery, black beans, and chickpeas in the Crock Pot.

2. Pour in the vegetable stock and stir in the tomato paste and bay leaf, basil, oregano, garlic, red pepper flakes, salt, and pepper.

3. Cover and cook for 5 hours and 30 minutes on low. Stir in the black olives and cook for an additional 30 minutes on low.

4. Take out the bay leaf and stir the stew to distribute the ingredients evenly. Ladle into soup bowls and top with fresh parsley. Serve with lime wedges.

Chicken and Peanut Stew

Number of Servings: 8

You'll Need:

- 12 pieces chicken legs
- 12 pieces chicken thighs
- 1 1/2 large yellow onion, peeled and sliced
- 3 bay leaves
- 3/4 tsp dried dill
- 6 cups chicken broth
- 2/3 cup peanut butter, creamy
- 4 Tbsp cornstarch
- 2/3 cup cold water
- Sea salt
- Freshly ground black pepper
- 2/3 cup finely chopped roasted peanuts

How to Prepare:

1. Combine the chicken legs and thighs in the Crock Pot, then season with the onion, dill, and bay leaf. Pour in the chicken broth, cover, and cook for 4 hours on low.

2. Take out the chicken and place on a covered dish. Remove the bay leaf from the pot.

3. Combine a ladleful of the soup from the slow cooker with the peanut butter and mix to combine. Pour the mixture into the Crock Pot.

4. Combine the water and cornstarch in a small bowl, then mix into the broth in the Crock Pot until thickened. Adjust seasoning to taste, if needed.

5. Arrange the chicken pieces on a deep platter and ladle the sauce on top. Sprinkle the chopped peanuts all over the dish. Best served on top of cooked rice.

Chapter 4: Chowders and Chilis

Bacon and Corn Chowder

Number of Servings: 6

You'll Need:

- 1 large red onion, chopped

- 6 bacon slices, diced

- 1/2 to 1 jalapeno chili, seeded and minced

- 1 clove garlic, minced

- 2/3 tsp salt

- 1/3 tsp pepper

- 3 Tbsp brown rice flour

- 1 1/2 lb red potatoes, peeled and diced

- 6 cups frozen sweet corn or canned sweet corn kernels, drained

- 3 cups half and half

- 6 cups chicken broth

- 4 Tbsp chopped fresh basil leaves

- 1 1/2 cups chopped cherry tomatoes

- Nonstick cooking spray

How to Prepare:

1. Place a skillet over medium flame and cook the diced bacon until crisp. Transfer into a lidded container and set aside.

2. Sauté the onion in the bacon fat until translucent, then stir in the garlic, jalapeno, salt, pepper, and flour. Sauté until flour becomes toasted.

3. Coat the Crock Pot with nonstick cooking spray and scrape the onion mixture into it. Pour in the corn, diced potato, and chicken broth. Stir to combine.

4. Cover and cook for 4 hours on high or for 8 hours on low.

5. An hour before the end of cooking time, add the half and half and stir. Adjust seasonings, if needed.

6. Ladle the chowder into soup bowls and top with the cooked bacon, fresh basil leaves, and cherry tomatoes.

Spicy Black Bean Chili

Number of Servings: 6

You'll Need:

- 1 1/2 Tbsp extra virgin olive oil
- 1 large red bell pepper, seeded and diced
- 1 1/2 large yellow onion, peeled and diced
- 3 cloves garlic, minced
- 3 Tbsp chili powder
- 36 oz canned crushed tomatoes
- 45 oz canned black beans, drained and rinsed
- 2 cups water
- 6 oz canned diced green chilies
- Sea salt
- Freshly ground black pepper

How to Prepare:

1. Combine the bell pepper, onion, and extra virgin olive oil in a microwaveable bowl. Cover and microwave for 1 minute on high. Stir in the chili powder and garlic and microwave for 30 seconds on high.

2. Pour the bell pepper mixture into the Crock Pot and stir in the beans, tomatoes, chilis, and water. Cover and cook for 8 hours on low.

3. Season to taste with salt and pepper, if needed, then serve.

Wild Rice and Pumpkin Chowder

Number of Servings: 6

You'll Need:

- 12 oz baby carrots
- 1 large potato, peeled and cubed
- 1 1/2 Tbsp olive oil
- 3/4 cup wild rice, rinsed and drained
- 3/4 lb beef sirloin tips
- 1 small onion, chopped
- 3 cloves garlic, minced
- 12 oz canned pumpkin
- 1 1/2 cups beef broth
- 3 cups water
- 3/4 tsp salt
- 3/4 Tbsp curry powder
- 1/6 tsp white pepper
- 1/3 cup heavy cream

How to Prepare:

1. Pour the carrots, wild rice, and diced potato into the Crock Pot.

2. Place a skillet over medium high flame and heat the olive oil. Sauté the beef until browned, then transfer into the Crock Pot with a slotted spoon.

3. Sauté the onion and garlic in the beef fat in the skillet until onion becomes translucent. Transfer with a slotted spoon into the Crock Pot.

4. Pour the broth and add the pumpkin into the skillet and cook, stirring constantly, to a simmer. Transfer into the Crock Pot.

5. Stir the water, salt, pepper, and curry powder into the Crock Pot. Cover and cook for 8 hours on low. Stir in the heavy cream and cook for an extra 15 minutes. Serve warm.

Vegan Chili

Number of Servings: 8

You'll Need:

- 3 Tbsp vegetable oil
- 1 large onion, diced
- 3 cloves garlic, minced
- 1 cup baby carrots, sliced
- 1 large green bell pepper, seeded and diced
- 24 oz canned pinto beans, undrained
- 24 oz canned red kidney beans, undrained
- 45 oz canned crushed tomatoes
- 1 1/2 lb firm tofu, rinsed and crumbled
- 3 cups water
- 3 cups frozen whole kernel corn, thawed
- 1 1/2 Tbsp cumin
- 1/3 tsp cayenne pepper
- 1 1/2 Tbsp chili powder
- Sea salt

How to Prepare:

1. Combine the green pepper, onion, carrot, and oil in the Crock Pot. Toss to coat. Cover and cook for half an hour on high.

2. Add the beans, garlic, tofu, crushed tomatoes, corn, cumin, chili powder, cayenne pepper, and a dash of salt. Mix well, then cover and cook for 2 hours on low or for 1 hour on high.

Creamy Cauliflower Chowder

Number of Servings: 8

You'll Need:

- 3 lb cauliflower florets
- 3 quarts vegetable stock
- 2 small onions, chopped
- 4 cloves garlic, minced
- 1 1/2 tsp white pepper
- 1/3 tsp sea salt
- 3 cups broccoli florets
- 2 celery stalks, diced
- 3 carrots, sliced into rounds

How to Prepare:

1. Combine the garlic, pepper, sea salt, cauliflower florets and vegetable stock into the Crock Pot. Mix well, then cook for 6 hours on low.

2. Use an immersion blender or food processor to puree the cauliflower. Return to the Crock Pot and stir in the celery, carrots, and broccoli.

3. Cover and cook for half an hour on low or until all the vegetables are fork tender.

Chapter 5: Red Meat Dishes

Pot Roast with Prune Gravy

Number of Servings: 6

You'll Need:

- 1 large clove garlic, minced
- 3/4 tsp crushed dried sage
- 1/8 tsp cayenne pepper
- 1/3 tsp sea salt
- 1/3 tsp freshly ground black pepper
- 2 1/2 lb boneless beef chuck roast
- 1 1/2 Tbsp olive oil
- 3/4 cup beef broth
- 1 medium onion, diced
- 3/4 cup pitted prunes, halved
- 3/4 lb parsnips, peeled and cubed
- 1 large apple, peeled, cored, thickly chopped
- 3/4 lb baby carrots
- 1/6 cup all purpose flour
- 1/6 cup butter
- 3/4 Tbsp balsamic vinegar

How to Prepare:

1. Combine the sage, garlic, cayenne, salt, and pepper in a bowl, then rub all over the beef.

2. Place a large skillet over medium high flame and heat the olive oil. Brown the roast all over, then transfer to the Crock Pot.

3. Pour the broth into the Crock Pot, coating the roast. Stir in the prunes, onion, apple, baby carrot, and parsnips. Cover and cook for 8 hours on low.

4. Move the roast and vegetables to a large platter and cover with aluminum foil.

5. Spoon the fat from the juices in the Crock Pot and stir in just enough water to make about a cup the liquid. Set Crock Pot to high, cover, and cook until bubbling.

6. In a small bowl, mix together the flour, butter, and a ladleful of the bubbling juices. Mix well, then pour the butter mixture into the Crock Pot. Stir constantly for about 12 minutes or until thickened. Season to taste with salt and pepper, then add the balsamic vinegar and stir.

7. Ladle the gravy all over the beef roast and vegetables and serve.

Lamb Shanks Cacciatore

Number of Servings: 8

You'll Need:

- 8 lamb shanks, 12 oz each
- 6 Tbsp olive oil
- 5 cloves garlic, minced
- 2 large sweet onions, diced
- 2 tsp coconut or maple sugar
- 1 cup dried porcini mushrooms
- 4 cups beef stock
- Juice from 4 oranges
- 6 Tbsp tomato paste
- 6 Tbsp chopped fresh rosemary or 2 Tbsp dried rosemary
- 4 Tbsp chopped fresh parsley
- 4 bay leaves
- 2 Tbsp cornstarch
- Sea salt
- Freshly ground black pepper

How to Prepare:

1. Preheat the broiler and line the pan with aluminum foil. Broil the lamb shanks until browned, about 3 minutes for each side.

2. Place the browned lamb shanks in the Crock Pot together with its juices from the pan.

3. Place a skillet over medium flame and heat the olive oil. Stir in the onion, salt, pepper, and sugar until onion is coated. Cover and cook for 10 minutes, stirring every now and then, to caramelize the onion.

4. Set heat to low and add the garlic. Saute until garlic becomes fragrant, then transfer to the Crock Pot.

5. As you cook the onion, take out a saucepan and mix together the beef stock and mushrooms. Place over high flame and bring to a boil, then turn off the heat and let the mushrooms soak for about 10 minutes. Use a slotted spoon to take out the mushrooms, then chop them up and pour into the Crock Pot. Strain the stock with a coffee filter into the Crock Pot.

6. Grate the zest from the oranges and add it into the Crock Pot together with the juices. Stir in the tomato paste, bay leaves, rosemary, and parsley.

7. Cover and cook for 10 hours on low or for 5 hours on high.

8. Combine the cornstarch with the cold water. Set Crock Pot heat to high and stir the cornstarch mixture into it until sauce thickens. Cook for 10 minutes, then remove the bay leaves.

9. Season to taste with salt and pepper, then transfer to a platter and serve.

Easy Barbecue Brisket

Number of Servings: 9

You'll Need:

- 2 1/2 lb beef brisket
- 2 Tbsp liquid smoke
- 1/2 cup chili sauce
- 1/4 cup barbecue sauce
- 1/4 tsp sea salt
- 1/8 tsp black pepper

How to Prepare:

1. Season the beef brisket liberally with salt, pepper, and liquid smoke. Place the brisket into the Crock Pot.

2. In a measuring cup, combine the chili and barbecue sauce very well. Pour on top of the brisket and turn to coat.

3. Cover and cook on low for 10 hours, or until the brisket is very tender. Shred with forks or slice with a knife. Best served as a sandwich filling.

Savory Beef and Eggplant

Number of Servings: 8

You'll Need:

- 1 1/2 lb eggplant, trimmed and diced
- 3 lb chuck roast, trimmed and sliced into bite sized cubes
- 2/3 cup olive oil
- 2 medium onions, chopped
- 5 cloves garlic, minced
- 2 green bell peppers, seeded and sliced thinly
- 2 cups dry red wine or apple cider
- 3 Tbsp balsamic vinegar
- 3 Tbsp light brown or coconut sugar
- 12 oz canned tomato sauce
- 5 Tbsp chopped fresh parsley
- 2 Tbsp chopped fresh marjoram or 2 tsp dried
- 3 bay leaves
- 3 tsp cornstarch
- 3 Tbsp cold water
- Sea salt
- Freshly ground black pepper

How to Prepare:

1. Season the eggplant cubes with salt in a colander, then place a plate and some cans on top of the eggplants to press and drain them for about half an hour. Rinse the eggplant cubes and press out excess water.

2. Preheat the oven broiler and line the pan with aluminum foil. Broil the beef until browned, about 3 minutes for each side. Place the beef into the Crock Pot along with its juices from the pan.

3. Place a skillet over medium flame and heat half of the olive oil. Sauté the onion, green pepper, and garlic until onion becomes translucent. Transfer to the Crock Pot.

4. Pour the rest of the olive oil into the skillet and set heat to medium high. Sauté the eggplant cubes until softened, then scrape into the slow cooker.

5. Stir the apple cider, sugar, balsamic vinegar, parsley, tomato sauce, bay leaves, and marjoram into the Crock Pot. Cover and cook for 8 hours on low or for 5 hours on high, or until all the ingredients are fork tender and cooked through.

6. Combine the cornstarch and cold water. Set heat to high and stir the cornstarch mixture into the Crock Pot. Cook for 15 minutes more, then take out the bay leaves.

7. Season to taste with salt and pepper, then serve.

Tropical Beef Ribs

Number of Servings: 6

You'll Need:

- 1 lb beef ribs, chopped into 6 pieces
- 2 potatoes, peeled and sliced into bite sized cubes
- 1 ear corn, husked and quartered
- 1 tomato, chopped
- 1 onion, chopped
- 1/2 green bell pepper, chopped
- 2 small bananas, peeled and sliced
- 2 cups beef broth
- 1/2 bunch cilantro, chopped
- 1/2 tsp dried oregano
- 1/4 tsp salt
- 1/4 tsp black pepper

How to Prepare:

1. Combine the chopped cilantro with the salt, pepper, and oregano.

2. Arrange the cut potatoes and corn in the Crock Pot and sprinkle a third of the cilantro seasoning all over.

3. Arrange the beef ribs on top of the potato and corn mixture and season with a third of the cilantro seasoning.

4. Arrange the chopped tomato, green pepper, and onion on top of the beef ribs, followed by the sliced bananas. Season with the remaining cilantro seasoning.

5. Pour in the broth, cover, and cook for 7 hours on low. Stir well to mix, then serve warm.

Chapter 6: Poultry and Pork Dishes

Jamaican Chicken Curry

Number of Servings: 6

You'll Need:

- 1 1/2 lb boneless, skinless chicken thigh, sliced into bite sized cubes
- 1/3 tsp ground nutmeg
- 1/3 tsp ground cloves
- 3/4 tsp ground ginger
- 3/4 Tbsp Madras curry powder
- 3/4 tsp allspice
- 3/4 tsp canola oil
- 1 small onion, chopped
- 1 large clove garlic, chopped
- 1 jalapeno, chopped
- 1/3 lb red skin potatoes, sliced into bite sized cubes
- 1/4 cup light coconut milk
- Nonstick cooking spray

How to Prepare:

1. Combine the allspice, cloves, nutmeg, ginger, and curry powder in a bowl. Place the chicken cubes into the bowl and turn several times to coat.

2. Place a skillet over medium flame and coat with nonstick cooking spray. Brown the chicken and transfer to the Crock Pot together with any remaining curry mixture.

3. Pour the canola oil into the skillet and heat over medium flame. Sauté the onion, pepper, and garlic until onion becomes translucent. Scrape into the Crock Pot.

4. Mix the potatoes and coconut milk into the Crock Pot. Cover and cook on low for 8 hours. Serve warm.

Oriental Pork Ribs

Number of Servings: 8

You'll Need:

- 5 lb country pork ribs, chopped into 8 pieces
- 1/3 cup hoisin sauce
- 2 cups ketchup or hoisin sauce
- 3 Tbsp soy sauce
- 3 Tbsp rice or white wine vinegar
- 3 Tbsp honey
- 1/3 tsp five spice powder
- 3 tsp minced fresh ginger
- 1 1/2 large sweet onions, diced
- 2 cloves garlic, minced
- 3 tsp toasted sesame oil
- Dried red pepper flakes

How to Prepare:

1. Combine the hoisin sauce, ketchup, vinegar, soy sauce, honey, five spice powder, ginger, onion, garlic, and sesame oil. Add a dash of dried red pepper flakes and mix well.

2. Arrange the pork ribs in the Crock Pot and pour the sauce all over. Turn several times to coat. Cover and cook for 8 hours on low.

3. Transfer the ribs onto a platter and pour the sauce on top. Serve warm.

Honey Glazed Turkey

Number of Servings: 6

You'll Need:

- 6 turkey legs, skinned
- 2/3 cup apricot jam
- 1 1/2 Tbsp fresh lemon juice
- 1 1/2 Tbsp soy sauce
- 1 1/2 Tbsp barbecue sauce
- 3 Tbsp honey
- 1 1/2 tsp paprika
- 1 1/2 tsp sea salt
- 1/3 tsp freshly ground black pepper
- 2/3 tsp dried thyme
- 2/3 tsp dried rosemary
- 1 1/2 tsp cold water
- 1 1/2 tsp cornstarch
- Nonstick cooking spray

How to Prepare:

1. Grease the Crock Pot with nonstick cooking spray. Set the heat to high and combine the honey, lemon juice, soy sauce, barbecue sauce, and apricot jam in it. Stir until thoroughly combined.

2. Add the paprika, rosemary, thyme, salt, and pepper into the Crock Pot and mix well. Place the turkey legs inside and turn several times to coat in the sauce.

3. Cover and cook for 8 hours on low. Remove the cover, set heat to high, and cook for an additional 30 minutes to thicken the sauce.

4. Take the turkey legs out of the Crock Pot using a pair of tongs and arrange on a platter. Cover with aluminum foil.

5. In a small bowl, mix together the water and cornstarch, then stir this into the Crock Pot together with the sauce. Stir constantly for 5 minutes until the sauce becomes a glaze, then pour all over the turkey legs. Serve warm.

Pork Adobo

Number of Servings: 6

You'll Need:

- 3/4 tsp canola oil
- 1 small onion, diced
- 3 cloves garlic, minced
- 2 1/2 lb pork loin
- 1 cup water
- 1/3 cup apple cider vinegar
- 1/6 cup orange juice
- 2 Tbsp light brown sugar
- 3/4 Tbsp ground Anaheim chili
- 3/4 Tbsp ground cumin
- 3/4 tsp ground cayenne pepper

How to Prepare:

1. Place a skillet over medium high flame and heat the canola oil. Brown the pork loin all over, then add the onion and garlic and saute until onion becomes translucent. Transfer the ingredients into the Crock Pot with a slotted spoon.

2. Add the water, vinegar, orange juice, sugar, chili, cumin, and cayenne into the Crock Pot and stir everything to combine. Cover and cook for 6 hours on low.

3. Transfer the pork onto a platter and shred using two forks. Pour the sauce all over and turn to coat. Best served with rice.

Italian Chicken and Potatoes

Number of Servings: 6

You'll Need:

- 6 boneless, skinless chicken breast halves

- 1/3 tsp dried oregano

- 1/3 tsp garlic salt

- 1/3 cup freshly grated Parmesan cheese

- 6 medium potatoes, sliced thickly

- 1 1/4 cups Italian salad dressing

How to Prepare:

1. Place a skillet over medium low flame and sauté the onion and sausage until sausage is browned. Crumble, drain, and scrape into the Crock Pot.

2. Combine the garlic and tomatoes with the sausage in the Crock Pot. Stir in the rice, coriander, cumin, saffron, white pepper, and sea salt.

3. Add the clam juice, chicken broth, and dry vermouth. Mix well. Cover and cook for 4 hours on low.

4. Place a skillet over medium flame and heat the olive oil. Cook the fish and shrimp until fish becomes flaky and shrimp becomes pink. Set aside. Scrub the clams and mussels and trim off the beards.

5. Add the green pepper, peas, fish, shrimp, clams, and mussels into the Crock Pot. Cook for an additional hour on low, discard unopened clams and mussels. Serve warm.

Halibut with Fennel and Tomatoes

Number of Servings: 8

You'll Need:

- 2/3 cup olive oil
- 3 medium fennel bulbs, stalks discarded
- 2 medium onions, sliced thinly
- 3 cloves garlic, minced
- 36 oz canned diced tomatoes, drained
- 3/4 cup dry white wine
- 3/4 cup freshly squeezed orange juice
- 1 1/2 Tbsp grated orange zest
- 1 1/2 Tbsp crushed fennel seeds
- 4 lb halibut fillets, sliced into 8 pieces
- Sea salt
- Freshly ground black pepper

How to Prepare:

1. Rinse the fennel and halve lengthwise, removing the top layer and core. Thinly slice.

2. Place a skillet over medium high flame and heat the olive oil. Saute the onion and garlic until onion becomes translucent. Stir in the fennel and cook for 2 minutes, then transfer the mixture into the Crock Pot.

3. Stir the tomatoes, orange juice and zest, wine, fennel seeds, and wine into the Crock Pot. Cover and cook for 7 hours on low or for 3 hours on high.

4. Season to the halibut with salt and black pepper, then set Crock Pot heat to high and place the fish over the fennel mixture. Cover and cook for 45 minutes.

5. Adjust seasoning to taste, if needed, then serve at once.

Chapter 7: Vegetable Dishes

Cheesy Vegetable Lasagna

Number of Servings: 6

You'll Need:

- 20 oz marinara sauce
- 10 oz canned diced tomatoes
- 6 oz package no boil lasagna noodles
- 10 oz ricotta cheese, part skim
- 6 oz shredded mozzarella cheese
- 8 oz frozen chopped spinach, thawed
- 3/4 cup frozen crumbled veggie burger, thawed
- Nonstick cooking spray

How to Prepare:

1. Combine the tomatoes and marinara in a bowl.

2. Grease the Crock Pot with the nonstick cooking spray, then pour about a third of the tomato marinara mixture into it. Layer a third of the noodles on top, overlapping the ends.

3. Pour third of the tomato marinara mixture on top, followed by about a third each of ricotta and mozzarella. Squeeze the thawed spinach dry, then layer half of it on top of the cheese.

4. Repeat the layers again, but adding the crumbled veggie burger in the second layer. The final layer should be the cheese.

5. Cover and cook for 3 hours on low. Slice and serve.

Farro Pilaf

Number of Servings: 8

You'll Need:

- 5 Tbsp olive oil
- 2 small onions, chopped
- 2 red bell peppers, seeded and chopped
- 1 celery stalk, minced
- 4 garlic cloves, minced
- 2 1/2 cups farro, rinsed
- 4 cups vegetable stock
- 8 oz canned diced tomatoes, undrained
- 2/3 cup oil cured black olives
- 2 bay leaves
- 1 1/2 Tbsp fresh thyme or 3/4 tsp dried thyme
- Sea salt
- Freshly ground black pepper
- 4 Tbsp chopped fresh parsley

How to Prepare:

1. Place a skillet over medium high flame and heat the oil. Sauté the onion, garlic, celery, and red bell pepper until onion becomes translucent. Transfer into the Crock Pot.

2. Stir the farro, olives, tomatoes, vegetable stock, bay leaves, and thyme into the Crock Pot. Mix well, then cover and cook for 7 hours on low or for 3 hours on high.

3. Take out the bay leaves, season to taste with salt and pepper. Mix in the parsley and serve immediately.

Vegetarian Moussaka

Number of Servings: 6

You'll Need:

- 2/3 cup dry yellow or brown lentils, rinsed and drained
- 3/4 cup water
- 1 1/2 large potatoes, peeled and cubed
- 1 celery stalk, diced
- 1 small sweet onion, diced
- 2 cloves garlic, minced
- 1/4 tsp salt
- 1/6 tsp ground cinnamon
- 1/6 tsp freshly ground black pepper
- 1/6 tsp dried oregano
- 1/6 tsp dried basil
- 1/6 tsp dried parsley
- Freshly ground nutmeg
- 1 small eggplant, cubed
- 8 baby carrots, sliced
- 10 oz canned diced tomatoes
- 6 oz cream cheese, softened
- 2 medium eggs

How to Prepare:

1. Combine the lentils, water, potatoes, celery, garlic, onion, cinnamon, salt, basil, pepper, parsley, oregano, and a dash of nutmeg in the Crock Pot. Mix well.

2. Arrange the eggplants on top, followed by the carrots. Cover and cook for 6 hours on low. Add the tomatoes and its juices and mix well.

3. Beat the eggs in a bowl and stir in the softened cream cheese. Spoon the egg mixture on top of the loaf, cover, and cook for an extra half hour. Let stand for Slice and serve.

Bulgur with Toasted Pine Nuts and Dried Fruit

Number of Servings: 8

You'll Need:

- 2 small onions, chopped
- 2 cloves garlic, minced
- 3 Tbsp olive oil
- 2 cups coarse or medium bulgur
- 3 cups vegetable stock
- 2 medium carrots, sliced thickly
- 1 1/2 cups chopped dried figs
- 3/4 cup pine nuts
- 2 inches cinnamon stick
- Sea salt
- Freshly ground black pepper
- 5 scallions, trimmed and chopped

How to Prepare:

1. Place a skillet over medium high flame and heat the oil. Sauté the onion and garlic until onion becomes translucent. Transfer to the Crock Pot.

2. Stir the bulgur, carrots, cinnamon stick, figs, and vegetable stock into the Crock Pot. Cover and cook for 6 hours on low or for 3 hours on high.

3. Toast the pine nuts in a dry skillet over medium flame until browned. Remove from heat.

4. Take the cinnamon stick out of the Crock Pot, then season to taste with salt and pepper. Spoon onto a platter and scatter the toasted pine nuts and chopped scallions on top. Serve at once.

Cauliflower and Potato Curry

Number of Servings: 6

You'll Need:

- 1/3 cup wheat berries
- 4 medium potatoes, peeled and quartered
- 2 cups water
- 1/2 cauliflower, sliced into florets
- 2/3 tsp ground turmeric
- 1/3 tsp chili powder
- 1 tsp ground cumin
- 1/3 tsp salt
- 1/6 tsp brown sugar
- 2 small tomatoes, chopped
- 1/3 tsp Garam Masala

How to Prepare:

1. Place the wheat berries into the Crock Pot. Boil a cup of water then pour directly on top of the wheat berries. Cover and cook for 1 hour on high.

2. Stir in the potatoes, cauliflower florets, turmeric, chili powder, cumin, salt, sugar, Garam Masala, tomatoes, and remaining water. Cover and cook on low for 6 hours.

3. Adjust seasoning to taste, if needed, then serve.

Chapter 8: Desserts

Tropical Coconut Banana Cake

Number of Servings: 6

You'll Need:

- 1/3 cup butter
- 1 cup granulated white sugar
- 6 oz cream cheese, softened
- 2 large eggs
- 1/3 cup heavy cream
- 3/4 Tbsp lemon juice
- 1 cup all purpose cake flour
- 1 1/2 small ripe bananas, sliced
- 1/3 tsp baking soda
- 3/4 tsp baking powder
- 1/6 tsp salt
- 1/3 cup unsweetened grated coconut
- 1/3 cup chopped pecans
- Nonstick cooking spray

How to Prepare:

1. Line the bottom of the Crock Pot with parchment paper and coat with nonstick cooking spray.

2. In a food processor, combine the cream cheese, butter, sugar, heavy cream, eggs, banana, and lemon juice. Pulse until thoroughly combined.

3. Mix in the flour, baking soda, salt, and baking powder. Mix the pecans and coconut into the batter.

4. Transfer the batter into the prepared Crock Pot, cover, and cook for 4 hours on low. Let it stand for 10 minutes before you slice and serve.

Raisin and Orange Rice Pudding

Number of Servings: 8 servings

You'll Need:

- 1 1/2 cups Arborio rice, rinsed well

- 4 cups water

- 1 1/2 cups coconut sugar

- 2 1/2 cups whole milk

- 1/3 tsp pure vanilla extract

- 2/3 cup orange marmalade

- 3 large eggs

- 2/3 cup raisins

- 1 1/2 cups heavy cream

- Sea salt

- Nonstick cooking spray

How to Prepare:

1. Combine the rice and water in the saucepan and add 3/4 cup coconut sugar and a dash of salt. Place over high heat and let boil for about 15 minutes, or until rice becomes fluffy. Drain and set aside.

2. Coat the Crock Pot with nonstick cooking oil, then transfer the rice into it. Add the milk, orange marmalade, vanilla, and remaining sugar. Beat the eggs and stir into the mixture together with the raisins.

3. Cover and cook for 5 hours on low or for 3 hours on high.

4. Take out the pudding from the Crock Pot and let stand to room temperature. Refrigerate for at least 1 hour to chill.

5. Place the heavy cream in a bowl in the refrigerator until chilled. Beat with an electric mixer until thick and peaks start to form. Combine whipped cream with the rice pudding and serve.

Carrot Cake

Number of Servings: 6

You'll Need:

- 1 cup all purpose flour
- 3/4 tsp baking powder
- 1/3 tsp baking soda
- 1/6 tsp salt
- 1/3 tsp cinnamon
- 1/6 tsp ground cloves
- 1/12 tsp freshly grated nutmeg
- 2 medium eggs
- 1/3 cup coconut sugar
- 1/4 cup butter
- 1/6 cup water
- 3/4 cup grated carrot
- Optional:
- 1/3 cup chopped walnuts
- Nonstick cooking spray

How to Prepare:

1. Combine the baking soda, salt, baking powder, flour, nutmeg, cloves, and cinnamon in a mixing bowl. Mix well.

2. Place the butter, sugar, and eggs in a food processor and mix until creamy. Transfer the egg mixture into the flour mixture and mix well.

3. Add the water and grated carrots into the mixture and mix well. Add the chopped walnuts and mix thoroughly.

4. Grease the Crock Pot with nonstick cooking spray, then transfer the batter into it, spreading it all out. Cover and cook for 2 hours on low. Let it stand for 10 minutes before you slice and serve.

Apple Bread Pudding

Number of Servings: 4 servings

You'll Need:

- 6 oz stale bread, cubed

- 3/4 lb Granny Smith apples, peeled, cored, and cubed

- 1/3 cup dried figs, stemmed and sliced thinly

- 2 large eggs

- 7 oz canned sweetened condensed milk

- 2 Tbsp melted unsalted butter

- 1 Tbsp freshly squeezed lemon juice

- 1 tsp grated lemon zest

- Salt

- Freshly grated nutmeg

- Optional: Sweetened whipped cream or yogurt or gelato

- Nonstick cooking spray

How to Prepare:

1. Coat the Crock Pot with nonstick cooking spray. Mix together the apples, figs, and cubed bread inside the Crock Pot.

2. In a bowl, beat the eggs and whisk in the melted butter, lemon juice and zest, condensed milk, and a dash of salt and nutmeg. Mix well, then pour into the Crock Pot.

3. Combine all of the ingredients in the Crock Pot, cover, and cook for 5 hours on low or for 2 hours on high.

4. Serve chilled or warm with sweetened whipped cream or yogurt or gelato on top, if desired.

Avocado Cake

Number of Servings: 6 servings

You'll Need:

- 1/3 cup butter
- 1 1/2 cups coconut sugar
- 2 eggs
- 1 1/2 avocado, pitted and peeled
- 2 cups cake flour
- 1/3 tsp allspice
- 1/3 tsp cinnamon
- 1/3 tsp salt
- 1 tsp baking soda
- 1/3 cup buttermilk
- 1/2 cup chopped pistachios
- 1/4 cup chopped dates
- 1/2 cup white raisins
- Optional: Confectioners' sugar

How to Prepare:

1. Mash together the coconut sugar and butter in a bowl. Whisk in the eggs, then mash in the avocado.

2. Sift the flour, salt, cinnamon, and allspice into a bowl.

3. Stir the baking soda into the buttermilk in a measuring cup, then slowly pour half into the avocado mixture, then half of the flour mixture, and so on until the flour and buttermilk are all incorporated into the avocado mixture.

4. Stir the dates, pistachios, and white raisins in to the batter. Coat the inside of a loaf pan with flour, then transfer the batter into it. Cover the top of the pan with aluminum foil, but not too tightly.

5. Put a rack inside the Crock Pot and place the loaf pan on top. Pour just enough water to reach the base of the rack. Cover the Crock Pot and cook for 2 hours on high.

Pressure Cooker Cookbook

Chapter 9: Pressure Cooking Explained

What Is Pressure Cooking?

An energy-saving method of cooking that does the job more quickly than traditional methods, pressure cooking uses a sealed container (pressure cooker) with water or other cooking liquids. The process does not allow liquids or air to escape under a pre-set pressure level.

Pressure cookers are able to quickly heat food because of the internal steam pressure that comes from the boiling water or liquid. This causes wet or saturated steam to permeate and bombard the food being cooked. The higher temperature of the water vapor allows faster transfer of heat (compared to dry air), and faster cooking. This reduces the amount of energy required to cook a particular dish because the water is not made to boil for a long time.

Upon reaching the target temperature, heat is lost only through the cooker's surface. Thus, pressure cooking is considered as the most efficient cooking method in terms of energy-efficiency.

Parts of a Pressure Cooker

Pressure cookers are usually made of stainless steel or aluminum. Aluminum models may be anodized, polished, or stamped, and are generally not dish-washer safe. They are also reactive to acidic foods, thus possibly altering the flavor of the dish being cooked. They are cheaper, and expectedly less durable than steel models.

Almost all portable pressure cookers today have the following parts and components, depending on the particular model and manufacturer:

Pan

- Metal body
- Pan Handle/s; some models have one handle; others have two, one on each side

Lid

- Lid handle, typically equipped with a locking mechanism (button or slider) that locks the cooker and prevents the lid from being removed while in use
- Sealing ring or gasket that seals the pressure cooker airtight

- Steam vent fitted with a pressure regulator at the top (either a spring device or weight) that maintains the pan's pressure level.
- Pressure indicator pin that indicates the absence or presence of pressure, no matter how slight
- Safety devices typically release valves for over pressure/over temperature pressure
- Pressure gauge that is normally seen in high-end models

Accessories – These usually include a steamer basket, a trivet to keep the steamer basket over the cooking liquid, and a metal divider that is used to separate food varieties in the steamer such as vegetables.

Chapter 10: Pressure Cooking Benefits

Pressure cookers have been used all over the world for a long time, although some people are still reluctant to use one. The hesitation may be due to some unpleasant childhood memories when using a pressure cooker came with some risks. In the past, aside from the screeching pressure cooker sound while in use, some models had the tendency to explode, sending the family's dinner to smithereens, splattered all over the kitchen and the ceiling.

Safety Features of Present-Day Pressure Cookers

The pressure cookers today are very safe to use and there is almost 0% possibility of exploding. Today's models also do not create the high-pitched, scary screeching sounds that came with the old versions. In addition, current pressure cookers are equipped with safety features that prevent buildup of excess pressure. Likewise, lid handle locks are designed not to open unless the pressure is released first. Simply put, present models are a far cry from the noisy, rattling, and steam-spewing pots that our grandparents are familiar with.

Pressure Cooking Benefits

A pressure cooker is a fixture in many kitchens today. It makes food preparation easier, and saves a lot of energy and time. Following are some of the major benefits you can expect from pressure cooking.

Food is tastier and retains most of the nutrients. – Food cooked using a pressure cooker offers more nutritional benefits than dishes cooked using traditional cooking methods for a longer period of time. This is because more nutrients are lost the longer a particular dish is cooked. On the other hand, it takes a significantly shorter amount of time to pressure cook, with less liquid or water used. Once the liquid is boiled away, the food is left with most of its nutrients intact.

Using a pressure cooker reduces typical cooking time by up to 70%. Traditional cooking methods require boiling food for a long time, and this causes the natural flavor of the ingredients to be steamed away. On the other hand, pressure cooking improves the natural flavor and richness of foods.

It saves a significant amount of energy. – One pressure cooker can do the job of several pots used on separate burners, and this translates to a considerable amount of energy savings. Many recipes can be cooked using the pressure cooker alone, and because various dishes are cooked much more quickly, less energy is used for cooking. With today's ever increasing cost of power, this is one great way to cut down on utility consumption.

It significantly cuts meal preparation time. – Pressure cooking reduces cooking time by as much as 70%. You can quickly whip up a delicious meal to feed a hungry family. Gone are the days when you get home from work with little energy left to cook, but you need to quickly put dinner on the table. A one-pot meal can easily be prepared with a pressure cooker. Your nutritious and delicious dinner will be ready in a matter of minutes. Just toss in the ingredients and by the time you finish setting up the table, dinner is ready to be served.

You enjoy a cooler kitchen. – With the record-setting number of heat waves sweeping most parts of the country in summer, having a cool kitchen is quite a relief. Cooking with traditional stove-top pans and pots produces heat that travels upwards. While some of the heat is sent out of the house through the stovetop fan, heat in the kitchen builds up as well. A pressure cooker, on the other hand, retains the steam and heat inside the cooker, allowing nothing to escape that can heat up the kitchen. This results to a cooler kitchen.

It requires less cleaning. – When cooking using traditional stove-top pots, you cannot help but leave residues on the control panel and stove-top, and at times, even on adjacent surfaces like counters and walls. This is due to the escaping steam and oils from the open cookware. All these require some time to clean up once the dish is done. On the other hand, a pressure cooker is safely secured with a lid that keeps unnecessary spatters and splashes from escaping the cooker. Likewise, the lid gets rid of possible boil overs that require additional cleaning. When the entire meal is done, you only have to wash one pot.

It can also be used for preserving food. – Pressure cooking can also be used to prepare foods intended for canning and to be kept for future consumption. This is why bigger models are also called "canners." These models can usually build pressure up to 15 psi, the required high pressure for cooking and canning of various foods like fish and meat. Smaller models can be utilized for home canning purposes as they hold a significantly lower amount than commercial models.

Chapter 11: Pressure Cooking Tips to Keep in Mind

After learning the benefits of pressure cooking and how it works, it is time to learn a few important adjustments you need to make on the traditional cooking methods you have gotten used to in order to optimize your use of the pressure cooker. Follow these tips and you are guaranteed to enjoy great pressure cooking results.

Put brown meats, poultry and veggies (such as carrots, peppers or chopped onions) first; then deglaze the cooker for more natural flavor. - Simply add some oil like canola or olive oil to the cooker without the lid, and heat over medium-high heat. Add small batches of food and cook until the food is brown all over. Transfer the food to a bowl and set it aside. Loosen up and take the tasty cooked-on juices and small food particles left by deglazing the cooker pot using a small amount of broth, wine, or even just plain water. Replace the cooked food inside the pot together with the rest of the ingredients. Allow to cook under pressure.

Evenly-sized pieces of food means food that is evenly cooked. – Cut the raw food into uniform-sized portions to make sore that they all cook evenly in a given amount of time.

Begin at high, and finish at low. – Begin pressure cooking at high heat. Once you reach the target pressure, bring the burner down to a simmer. You do not have to worry about heat adjustments when using an electric pressure cooker as it automatically does it for you.

Avoid overdoing the liquid. – Because the food is cooked under pressure in a sealed pot, there is less evaporation. It follows that less cooking is liquid compared to cooking using conventional means. It is important, however, to make sure that there is enough liquid, regardless of the dish you are preparing. 1 cup of liquid is usually a good rule of thumb to follow, but to be sure, check the user's manual or refer to the recipe book to find out exactly how much liquid the product manufacturer recommends. Never, under any circumstances, fill the cooker with liquid in excess of half of its full capacity.

Never load the cooker with an excessive amount of food. – Do not fill up over 2/3 of the pressure cooker capacity with food or ingredients. Likewise do not tightly pack food in the cooker. Ignoring this all-important pressure cooking guideline may result to the inefficient operation of your pressure cooker, possibly affecting the quality of the finished product. It may also trigger the activation of he built-in safety mechanisms of the cooker, particularly if there is a large amount of food in the cooker.

For best results, use the stop-and-go cooking method. – When doing a recipe that has ingredients requiring varying cooking times, start by putting slow to cook ingredients like meats first. To stop cooking, apply the quick-release method. Add the easy to cook ingredients like peas or green beans next. Bring the pressure back up and finish cooking the entire dish at the same time.

Avoid burning when using a stove-top pressure cooker by playing burner hopscotch. – Upon reaching pressure at high heat, adjust the burner down to a simmer. Most gas burner models quickly react, but not most electric models. If you are using an electric stove, you can use 2 burners, one at high heat to achieve pressure and the other at low setting for maintaining pressure. Switch to the low setting burner once pressure is reached.

Set the timer. – Keep a kitchen timer within reach so that once the cooker achieves and maintains the target pressure, you can easily set it for the recipe-specified cooking time. Some electric pressure cooker models have a built-in digital timer.

It may take a longer time to cook at high altitude. – If you live in a high-altitude area, you may need to adjust your cooking time, especially if you are at 3,000 ft. above sea level, at least. Follow the generally-accepted rule of thumb, which is to increase cooking times by 5% for every 1000 ft. in excess of 2,000 ft. above sea level.

Release the pressure. – When you are done pressure cooking, use the appropriate method to release pressure, depending on the recipe you are working on.

Chapter 12: Pressure Cooker Recipes: Meat Dishes

Beef Dishes

Pressure Cooker Corned Beef

An all-time family favorite, corned beef is simple and quite easy to prepare, more so when pressure cooked. It will also remain good for a long period of time when refrigerated. In addition, leftovers can be recycled to make tasty sandwiches, or served with other dishes next time.

Makes 6 servings

Preparation Time: 1 hour

Cooking Time: 1 hour

Ingredients:

- 2 kgs. corned beef brisket (flat-cut)
- 340 grams sliced celery
- 2 small unpeeled and sliced oranges
- 2 small thinly sliced onions
- 2 chopped garlic cloves
- 3 halved bay leaves
- 1 tbsp. dill

- 4 halved cinnamon sticks
- 500 ml water

Instructions:

1. Soak the beef brisket in water for about an hour. Drain immediately before cooking.
2. Place the beef brisket in the pressure cooker. If the meat is too big, divide it in half. Add all the other ingredients. Put just enough water to cover the meat surface.
3. Put the lid in place and lock. Put the pressure regulator properly on the vent pipe then turn on the heat to medium.
4. Allow the meat to cook for 50 minutes at 15 psi. The pressure regulator must be slowly rocking while cooking.
5. Apply the natural release method before removing the cooker from the heat and waiting for pressure to go down.
6. Carefully take the lid off, and then transfer the meat to a serving platter. Allow it to rest for about 5 minutes.
7. Slice the meat thinly, against the grain. Serve.

Chili con Carne

In just 60 minutes, you can indulge in a hot bowl of chili con carne easily prepared through pressure cooking. This is a very popular recipe the world over. A warm bowl of the dish can easily wash all your blues away. It is ideal for lunch, dinner, or as a snack on a rainy and lazy afternoon. This recipe is a healthy version. Low in sodium, but just as delectable. Serve it with rice, bread, or biscuits.

Makes 4 servings
Preparation Time: 30 minutes
Cooking Time: 30 minutes

Ingredients:

- 400 grams ground beef
- 4 tbsps. olive oil
- 1 bay leaf
- 1 chopped medium onion
- 2 finely chopped garlic cloves
- 150 grams of soaked kidney beans
- 300 grams of drained & chopped canned tomatoes
- 1 tsp tomato paste
- 1 tsp salt
- 1 tbsp chili powder
- dried basil leaves

- 1/2 tsp ground cumin
- 180 ml water

Instructions:

1. Heat one tablespoon of olive oil in the pressure cooker without the lid for 2 minutes. Allow the ground beef to cook until it turns brown before removing from the uncovered cooker.
2. Put the rest of the oil. Add the garlic and onions and stir fry until they turn light brown.
3. Toss in the beef together with the other ingredients. Stir.
4. Place the pressure cooker lid and lock. Bring the heat to high. Once the target pressure is reached, lower the heat and allow to cook for about 18 minutes.
5. Take the cooker away from the heat and allow it to cool on its own.
6. Remove the bay leaves. Serve the dish hot.

Beef Pot Roast

With this dish, dinnertime is worth looking forward to, particularly when you are coming home from a long and tiring day at the office. There is no better way to relieve your rumbling tummy and unpleasant mood than with the inviting aroma and mouth-watering taste of a perfectly done pot roast? This quick and easy to cook dish is for the whole family to enjoy.

Makes 6 to 8 servings

Preparation Time: 10 minutes

Cooking Time: 1 hour

Ingredients:

- 1.5 to 1.75 kg beef chuck roast
- 118 ml red wine
- 500 ml beef stock
- ½ tsp chicken salt
- ½ tsp smoked paprika
- ½ tsp salt
- ½ tsp black pepper
- 1 roughly chopped medium onion
- 5 chunked medium potatoes
- 4 minced garlic cloves
- 3 chunked medium carrots

Instructions:

1. Prepare the beef by trimming the excess fat off.
2. Combine the salt, paprika, black pepper and chicken salt in a small-sized bowl.
3. Thoroughly rub the salt mixture on the beef.
4. Put the beef in the pressure cooker.
5. Add the onions, garlic, red wine, and beef stock.
6. Lock the pressure cooker lid and cook for 45 to 50 minutes at high pressure.
7. Remove the cooker from the heat and apply the quick release method.
8. Check the beef for tenderness.
9. Add the carrots and potatoes; make sure to evenly distribute the veggies inside the pot.
10. Bring to pressure and allow to cook for another 5 to 10 minutes.
11. Apply the natural release method. Remove the lid and serve warm with gravy.

Pasta Casserole

You can never put a good Italian pasta dish down. The pressure cooker is used for most of the required cooking for this dish. A little help is required from your grill just for the cheese to provide the perfect crunch. This dish is perfect for the whole family to enjoy on a cold winter night.

Makes 4 servings

Preparation Time: 15 minutes

Cooking Time: 20 minutes

Ingredients:

- 500 g Rigatoni pasta
- 300 g ground beef
- 375 g shredded Mozzarella cheese
- 450 g tomato puree
- 1 celery stalk
- 1 carrot
- 1 onion
- 25 ml red wine
- salt & pepper
- butter

Instructions:

1. Pre-heat the uncovered pressure cooker at medium heat.

2. Chop the celery, onions, and carrots.

3. Add butter (around 2 tbsps.) Cook the celery, onions, and carrots for about 5 minutes or until the soften.

4. Turn up the heat to high. Put the ground beef in the cooker followed by a pinch of salt & pepper.

5. Allow to cook for about 10 minutes or until the meat turns brown on all sides.

6. After all the water has evaporated and the meat starts to sizzle, deglaze the pan by adding some wine. Cook some more to allow the wine to evaporate, which should only take about a minute.

7. Add the tomato puree and the pasta. If desired, season with salt. Pour enough water to fully cover the pasta. Then start stirring and flattening the pasta. Use as small amount of water as possible.

8. Set the cooker at low pressure and the heat at high. Upon reaching the pressure, lower the heat and allow to cook for 5 minutes more.

9. Release the pressure, and unlock the lid.

10. Stir the pot contents, allowing the pasta some time to rest.

11. Transfer half of the cooked contents to an oiled deep dish or casserole. Sprinkle some shredded cheese on top. Pour the remaining contents of the cooker on top, and sprinkle with the rest of the shredded cheese.

12. If desired, pat or brush with butter.

13. Put the casserole under the casserole for 3 minutes or just enough time to melt the cheese and achieve a golden color.
14. Serve hot and enjoy!

Additional Notes:

1. You can use biscuits or other available crumbs for the crust.
2. If you notice condensed water resting on the food after removing it from the cooker, blot it gently using a paper towel.
3. You can serve the dish topped with nutmeg, cinnamon, a dollop of whipped cream, or simply on its own.

Pork Dishes

Boneless Pork Roast w/ Fennel

No meat-lover can resist this flavorful and succulent dish. This succulent and aromatic dish, with the meticulous preparation it demands, is a big hit for lunch or dinner. The best part is that you can prepare this dish in only two hours with the help of a pressure cooker – this is a lot quicker than whipping up the dish using traditional cooking methods.

Makes 4 servings

Preparation Time: 20 minutes

Cooking Time: 1 hour 20 minutes

Ingredients:

- 2 tbsps. olive oil
- 1 kilo boneless pork
- salt & ground pepper, to taste
- 1 sliced onion
- 2 cloves of peeled & crushed garlic
- 150 ml chicken stock
- 150 ml white wine
- ½ kg thickly sliced fennel bulbs

Instructions:

1. Put olive oil in the pressure cooker (heavy based) at high heat.

2. Add the pork seasoned w/ a pinch of salt & pepper; cook until a brown color is achieved on all sides.

3. Transfer the roast from the heat into a plate. Set it aside for a while.

4. Put the garlic into the cooker, followed by the chicken stock and white wine. Bring it to a boil. Using a wooden spoon, scrape the bottom to retrieve the juices.

5. Put the roast back into the pressure cooker. Cover it and let it cook for 35 to 40 minutes.

6. Carefully remove the pressure cooker lid to add the fennel and sliced onion.

7. Place the lid again and cook for another 15 minutes or just until the veggies tenderize.

8. Get the cooker out of the heat. Remove the roast and vegetables. Keep everything warm using a separate dish.

9. Put the pressure cooker back at medium heat, uncovered. Wait a few minutes to let the sauce cook. If you prefer sticky and thicker sauce, add a tsp. of flour, then stir constantly.

10. Serve the roast along with the sauce and fennel mix.

Pork Loin w/ Veggies

Perfectly roasted pork loin paired with fresh and crisp veggies – heavenly! This pressure cooker recipe introduces an exciting and savory new way to enjoy the popular dish. With its enhanced flavor, there is no wonder you will come back for a second serving.

Makes 4 servings
Preparation Time: 15 minutes
Cooking Time: 45 minutes

Ingredients:

- 900 grams boneless top roast pork loin
- 250 ml water
- 3 sliced carrots
- 6 garlic cloves
- 3 quartered potatoes
- 1 quartered onion
- salt & pepper
- 2 sliced celery stalks
- 1 bay leaf
- 2 tbsps. of vegetable oil

Instructions:

1. Using a paring knife, slit the pork loin on top, about 2 to 3 cm. deep.
2. Cut a hole in between the slits, big enough to insert the garlic cloves. Push the cloves entirely into the meat.
3. To taste, season with salt & pepper.
4. Put the vegetable oil and cook the pork at medium high heat. Allow to cook until all the sides are browned.
5. Drain the excess oil after cooking.
6. Put the water in the pot. (Do this only after the cooker cools down.)
7. Put the bay leaf.
8. Put the pork on the trivet or cooking rack.
9. Put the lid w/ the pressure regulator securely on the vent pipe.
10. Allow to cook at 15 psi for half an hour.
11. After 30 minutes, cool the cooker immediately and take the meat out.
12. Put the veggies on the trivet or rack.
13. Put the meat back on top of the veggies.
14. Securely close the lid with the regulator on the vent.
15. Allow to cook at 15 psi for 5 minutes more.
16. Immediately allow the cooker to cool down then take the meat and veggies out.
17. Allow the meat to rest for about 5 minutes. Carve and serve.

Additional Notes:

1. To fully maximize the flavor of the veggies, chop them into 2 to 3 cm pieces.

2. You can adjust the number of garlic holes to achieve the level of garlic flavor you prefer.

3. Make sure that each time you put the pressure cooker lid, the contents do not exceed 2/3 of the cooker's full capacity.

4. After the dish is done, use the remaining liquids in the cooker as sauce.

Char Siu (Chinese-Style Pork Barbecue)

Everyone loves barbecue parties. This dish is perfect for a weekend BBQ party with family and friends. But instead of the good old-fashioned grill, the dish is cooked with a pressure cooker. Best served green veggies, rice, and barbecue sauce, this is great barbecue with a twist.

Makes 6 servings

Preparation Time: 15 minutes

Cooking Time: 50 minutes

Ingredients:

- 1 kg trimmed pork belly
- 4 tbsps soy sauce
- 1 liter chicken stock
- 8 tbsps. of char siu sauce (you can get it in Asian food/deli stores)
- 2 tbsps honey
- 1 tsp peanut oil
- 2 tbsps dry sherry
- 2 tsps sesame oil

Instructions:

1. Mix the soy sauce, stock, sherry, and ½ of the prepared char siu sauce at medium heat in the pressure cooker with lid off.
2. Allow to cook for 5 to 8 minutes.
3. Put the pork belly in. Place the lid on and bring to the target pressure. Reduce the heat to medium for half an hour more.
4. Let the cooker cool down naturally.
5. Take the pork out and let it cool down. Do not throw away the remaining cooking liquid.
6. Chop the cooked pork belly into even-sized pieces.
7. Heat the peanut oil in a frying pan at medium high heat. Let the pork cook.
8. Mix the sesame oil, honey, and the remaining char siu sauce in a separate bowl.
9. Use the mix to brush the pork belly pieces while cooking for ten minutes or until it is fully coated and brown.
10. Pour the leftover cooking liquid in a saucepan and cook it at medium high heat.
11. Allow it to boil before reducing the heat. Simmer for about 3 minutes.
12. Pour the mixture over the pork. Serve and enjoy.

Lamb Dishes

Lamb Shanks

Tender and with meat falling off the bone, perfectly cooked lamb shanks ready to eat in only half an hour. This dish is the perfect dinner for the whole family after a long day at work or school. Pressure cooking makes this dish even more tender and savory.

Makes 4 servings

Preparation Time: 15 minutes

Cooking Time: 45 minutes

Ingredients:

- 4 lamb shanks
- 2 tbsps olive oil
- 60 g plain flour
- 1 chopped large onion
- 3 large carrots, chopped into medium-sized pieces
- 1 tsp oregano
- 2 tbsps of tomato paste
- 2 crushed garlic cloves
- 1 quartered medium tomato
- 1 beef bouillon cube
- 60 ml water
- 180 ml red wine
- salt & pepper

Instructions:

1. Put all the flour in a shallow container then add a dash of salt & pepper. Mix.
2. Roll the shanks in the mixture to coat.
3. Put olive oil in the cooker and heat at medium to high setting.
4. Allow the lamb shanks to brown in the hot oil before transferring to a plate.
5. Use the same oil to sauté the crushed garlic, chopped onion, carrots, and oregano for 4 to 5 minutes or until the slices of onion are translucent.
6. Place the quartered tomato, tomato paste, water, bouillon cube, and red wine.
7. Stir and allow to boil before putting back the lamb shanks in.
8. Place the lid and lock. Bring until the desired pressure is achieved.
9. Reduce the heat to low and continue cooking for another 20 to 25 minutes.
10. Use the natural method to release the pressure.
11. Take the lamb shanks out of the cooker and transfer to a serving dish.
12. Serve and enjoy!

Additional Notes:

If you want your gravy thicker, mix 1 ½ tbsps. of water with 2 tbsps. of plain starch to create a paste. Once the lamb is removed from the cooker, stir the paste into the leftover sauce. Serving the dish with some fluffy mashed potatoes is highly recommended.

Lamb Barley Stew

Comfort food comes in various forms, depending on personal preference – fried chicken, soups, desserts, steak, and many others. If you want to try something new, but hearty and delicious, nonetheless, try this pressure cooked stew dish that is sure to satisfy your cravings and fill your tummy!

Makes 4 servings

Preparation Time: 20 minutes

Cooking Time: 45 minutes

Ingredients:

- 1 cooked leg of lamb, cooked
- 200 g barley
- 5 carrots
- 150 g frozen peas
- 3 onions
- 500 ml water
- 250 ml beef broth

Instructions:

1. Separate the lamb meat from the leg bone. Cut into bite-size pieces.
2. Put the bone in the cooker.
3. Put some water, broth, and barley into the pressure cooker.

4. Cook with the lid on at high heat.

5. Upon reaching the desired high pressure, reduce the heat just enough to maintain the pressure. Allow to cook for 20 minutes more.

6. Release the pressure once the cook time is over.

7. Remove the lid. Take the bone out of the cooker. Put back the residual meat that stuck to the bone back into the cooker.

8. Put the quartered onions and sliced carrots into the pressure cooker.

9. Cook for 10 minutes more at high heat.

10. Release the pressure once cooked.

11. Add the meat and peas.

12. Serve and enjoy!

Additional Notes:

1. Leftover lamb meat is great for this recipe. Any type of red meat like beef or pork can also be used.

2. If preferred, you can add more vegetables to the dish like green beans and tomatoes.

3. If beef broth is not available, you can replace it with 2 bouillon cubes. Just make sure to add 250 ml of water.

4. You can adjust the water to beef broth ratio, depending on your preference.

Chapter 13: Pressure Cooker Recipes – Fish and Seafood Dishes

Fish Chowder

On their own, chowders are hearty, delicious and filling meals. However, they also make great starters or sides. Here is a tasty fish chowder recipe, made easier to prepare using your pressure cooker.

Makes 4 to 6 servings

Preparation Time: 15 minutes

Cooking Time: 25 minutes

Ingredients:

- 500 g skinless and boneless haddock or another type white fish, sliced into medium chunks
- 350 g washed and peeled potatoes, chopped into medium-sized chunks
- 350 ml milk
- 450 ml water
- 1 finely chopped small onion,
- 470 ml chicken stock
- 470 ml half & half (4 parts of whole milk w/ 1 part heavy cream)
- Salt & pepper, to taste

Instructions:

1. Put the fish chunks, chicken stock, milk, and water into the pressure cooker.

2. Cover the cooker and lock the lid; bring to pressure at medium-high heat. Allow to cook for another 8 to 10 minutes once pressure is reached.

3. Take the cooker away from the heat and naturally release the pressure.

4. Carefully open the cooker and without the pressure cooker lid, bring the heat to medium low.

5. Add some salt & pepper to taste.

6. Stir the half & half in and stir continuously until the chowder has thickened slightly.

7. Remove the cooker from the heat. Garnish the dish as desired.

8. Serve and enjoy!

Mediterranean Style Fish

You will find this dish unique if you have been accustomed to pairing steamed fish with lemon. This recipe calls for a combination of capers and tomatoes for a tasty, but at the same time sweet, and somewhat vinegary end result.

Makes 4 servings

Preparation Time: 5 minutes

Cooking Time: 10 minutes

Ingredients:

- 4 fillets of white fish
- 500g halved cherry tomatoes
- 1 pressed clove of garlic
- 2 tbsps. of pickled capers
- 1 cup of Taggiesche olives
- thyme
- olive oil
- salt & pepper (optional)

Instructions:

1. Put the cherry tomato halves at pit of a heat-proof bowl.
2. Put in some fresh thyme.
3. Top the tomatoes with the fish.
4. Add the olive oil, crushed garlic, and a pinch of salt.

5. Put everything including the bowl inside the cooker.

6. Turn up the heat to high, and set the pressure cooker to low. After reaching pressure, lower the heat and allow to cook for 5 more minutes.

7. Once the cooking time is over, release the pressure using the natural method.

8. Serve individually in separate plates. Garnish with more herbs and cherry tomatoes on top. Enjoy!

Octopus and Potatoes

Tough and rubbery consistency – this is probably the first thing that comes to your mind upon hearing about an octopus dish, right? Add the fact that it is difficult to prepare and cook, and not to mention eat! However, there is a secret to properly tenderizing the flesh prior to cooking. Not too many people are aware of that, and this recipe will let you in on that big secret!

Makes 6 servings

Preparation Time: 20 minutes

Cooking Time: 35 minutes

Ingredients:

- 1 kg octopus
- 3 garlic cloves
- 1 kg potatoes
- chopped parsley
- 1 bay leaf
- 125 ml olive oil
- 1/2 tsp peppercorns
- 5 tbsps vinegar
- salt & pepper

Instructions:

1. To clean the octopus properly, remove the head, halve the body and then turn it inside out. Remove everything inside, including the eyes. Find the area where the tentacles meet and take out the beak. Put under running water to rinse. Then set it aside.

2. Thoroughly wash the potatoes and put them in the pressure cooker unpeeled. Add just enough water to cover half of the potatoes then season w/ salt.

3. Place the lid and lock. Set the heat to high. When the pan starts to whistle, lower the burner to medium low. Allow to cook for 15 minutes at this temperature.

4. Release the vapor afterwards. Using tongs, take the potatoes out. Do not discard the remaining cooking water.

5. Using a fork and tongs, peel the potatoes. Put some water just enough to almost cover the octopus entirely.

6. Add the bay leaf, pepper, a pinch of salt and a clove of garlic. Bring to a boil.

7. Put the octopus in the pressure cooker, tentacles first.

8. Put the lid and lock. Allow to cook at high heat until pressure is reached. Afterwards, lower the heat to minimum temperature, just enough to maintain the pressure. Let it cook for another 20 minutes.

9. When done coking, release pressure then open the cooker carefully. By this time, the octopus flesh should have

enough tenderness to allow a fork to easily sink through. If not, cook for 2 or 3 minutes more.

10. Strain off the liquids. Chop the octopus flesh into bite-size pieces and set aside.

11. Mix the vinegar, olive oil, salt & pepper, and crushed garlic cloves in a small container or jar then seal. Thoroughly shake to blend all the flavors together. This mixture will be your vinaigrette.

12. By now, the potatoes should have cooled down. Chop them into chunks the same size of the octopus.

13. Mix all the ingredients in a bowl. Put chili, chopped parsley on top. Tightly cover the bowl then refrigerate before serving.

Additional Notes:

1. If desired, remove the skin of the octopus using the backside of a knife before serving.

2. You can use other spices and herbs you want to season and garnish the cooked dish.

3. If you don't have enough time to cook, you can cook the octopus and the potatoes at the same time, but this will make the potatoes purplish in color because of the skin of the octopus seeping into the cooking liquid.

4. For best results, tenderize the octopus before cooking, particularly if bought fresh. This can be done by storing it in the freezer for one whole day before defrosting.

Salmon Al Cartoccio

In Italian, al cartoccio directly translates to packet cooking. It is called en pallion in France. Basically, it is a way to cook fish by steaming in its own zest and juices, with some veggies on the side. This is a good way to cook fish, but since it is very delicate, it must be protected from the turbulence of the pressure cooker. Thus, the fish is thoroughly wrapped in oven paper or foil or both.

Makes 4 servings
Preparation Time: 20 minutes
Cooking Time: 15 minutes

Ingredients:

- 4 fresh or frozen salmon fillets
- 3 sliced tomatoes
- 1 shaved white onion
- 1 sliced lemon
- 4 sprigs of thyme
- 4 sprigs of parsley
- olive oil
- salt & pepper, to taste

Instructions:

1. Arrange all the ingredients on parchment paper using this order – swirl of oil, 1 potato layer, salt & pepper and oil, fish fillet, salt & pepper and oil, herbs and onion rings, slices of lemon, salt, and oil.

2. Next, fold the packet and wrap it in tinfoil snugly.

3. Pour 2 cups of water into the pressure cooker. Put the steamer basket in proper position then lay the packet on top.

4. Cook 2 fillets at a time. If your cooker is tall or large enough, you can use 2 layers of baskets simultaneously.

5. Seal the pressure cooker with its lead. Set to high heat and wait until target pressure is reached. Turn the heat down to minimum setting.

6. The cooking time should be in the vicinity of 12 to 15 minutes. You can release the vapor afterwards, but don't open the top just yet.

7. Allow the fish packets to sit inside the locked cooker for about 5 minutes more.

8. Carefully open the cooker and take the packets out. Remove the tinfoil. Serve and enjoy!

Additional Notes:

1. This fish recipe is ideal for any drained and thawed white fish fillet such as grouper.
2. You can replace lemons with white wine.
3. If you want, you can experiment with various spices and herbs.
4. Make sure there is enough spacing between packets when cooking.
5. To achieve the desired thin slices of onions and potatoes, use a mandolin slicer.

Coconut Fish Curry

Curry dishes are distinctly Indian cuisine, even with all the different versions in terms of cooking style and ingredients. The pair of fish and coconut is probably the top favorite in the world to cook with earthly spices and herbs. This is best illustrated with this pressure cooker recipe version of the rich and spicy classic Indian dish that is prefect for dinner or lunch.

Makes 6 to 8 servings

Preparation Time: 5 minutes

Cooking Time: 15 minutes

Ingredients:

- 750 g fish fillets, rinsed and cut in bite-size pieces
- 500 ml coconut milk (unsweetened)
- 1 chopped tomato
- 2 capsicums, sliced into strips
- 2 squeezed garlic cloves
- 6 curry leaves
- 2 onions, sliced into strips
- 2 tsps of ground cumin
- 1 tbsp of ground coriander
- 1/2 tsp of ground turmeric
- 1 tbsp of freshly grated ginger
- 1 tsp of hot pepper flakes

- 1/2 tsp of ground fenugreek
- lemon juice
- salt

Instructions:

1. Pre-hat the cooker at medium low without cover.
2. Put the oil and the curry leaves then fry for one minute.
3. Add the garlic, ginger, and onion. Sauté until tender.
4. Put the 5 ground spices (cumin, coriander, fenugreek, hot pepper, and turmeric.) Together with the onions, sauté for 2 minutes.
5. To deglaze, add the coconut milk. Make sure that nothing remains stuck to the cooker's bottom.
6. Add the fish, tomatoes, and capsicum. Stir to make sure that the fish is coated with the mixture very well.
7. Set the level of heat to high, and the pressure level to low. Upon reaching pressure, turn down the heat to low.
8. Cook at low pressure for 5 minutes.
9. Release the vapor to release the pressure.
10. To taste, season with salt then spritz the dish on top with lemon juice.

Additional Notes:

1. If unavailable, you can substitute fresh fish with frozen or thawed fish.

2. A good alternative to tomatoes is 1 cup of cherry tomatoes.

3. If fresh ginger is not available, you can replace it with 1/8 tsp. of ginger powder.

4. For curry leaves, good alternatives are basil, bay leaves or kaffir lime leaves.

5. In lieu of hot pepper flakes, you can opt to use chili powder.

6. For the 5 spices, you can use 3 tablespoons of curry powder mix.

Chapter 14: Pressure Cooker Recipes – Vegetarian Dishes

Pumpkin Soup

Halloween is the time of year when people have a great time making horrifying or fun jack-o-lantern faces but once the occasion is over, what remains are chunks of pumpkins that need to be consumed. So, what can you do other than the usual pie? That's it: pumpkin soup. Here is an easy to prepare dish using your pressure cooker. Add bay leaves and grated apple into the mix and what do you get? Pumpkin soup that is delicious in its own subtle way!

Makes 12 servings

Preparation Time: 25 minutes

Cooking Time: 25 minutes

Ingredients:

- 1 tbsp butter
- Butternut pumpkin chunks
- 1 diced potato
- 1 peeled, cored and grated apple
- 1 chopped brown onion
- 4 bay leaves
- 750 ml of chicken stock

- Cracked black pepper
- Curry powder
- 500 ml milk

Instructions:

1. Melt the butter in the cooker.
2. Add the chunks of pumpkin, onion, potato, and a bit of curry powder. Cook at low heat gently until the onion slightly turns brown while occasionally stirring.
3. Next, add the chicken stock, bay leaves, and black pepper.
4. Seal the pressure cooker before bringing to pressure. Allow to cook for about 5 minutes.
5. Use the cold water method to release pressure.
6. Stir the grated apple in, and cook for 10 minutes without the pressure cooker cover. Stir occasionally.
7. Take the bay leaves out. Transfer the remaining contents of the cooker into a blender. Process. Add some milk until the soup is smooth and creamy.
8. Serve warm in bowls. The soup is best served with croutons.

Vegetarian Chili

Chili is easily one of the Mexican foods popular the world over. With its spicy, delectable goodness, it warms the heart and fills the tummy. This dish will keep you going on a cold day. With this pressure cooker recipe, you will get not only the full chili flavor without the meat, but you get to enjoy this Mexican dish in less than 30 minutes. That's amazing considering that beans take a lifetime to soften using traditional cooking methods.

Makes 6 to 8 servings

Preparation Time: 15 minutes

Cooking Time: 30 minutes

Ingredients:

- 225 grams pinto beans (soaked overnight prior to cooking)
- 225 grams red kidney beans (soaked overnight prior to cooking)
- 375 grams roughly chopped Roma tomatoes
- 900 ml water
- 2 roughly chopped onions
- 1 pack ground round Yves veggie
- 3 minced garlic cloves, minced
- 1 diced capsicum, diced
- 2 tsps cumin
- 1 bay leaf

- 2 tbsps of olive oil
- 1 ½ tsps oregano
- 1 tbsp chilli powder(put more if spicier chili is preferred)
- Salt, to taste

Instructions:

1. At medium setting, heat olive oil in the cooker.
2. Sauté the garlic cloves and onions until translucent.
3. Add the ground round veggie and cook until brown. Then toss in the cumin, capsicum, oregano, chili powder, salt, and bay leaf. Mix everything well.
4. Add the beans, water, and tomatoes. Stir.
5. Cover the pressure cooker and lock. Bring to pressure and allow to cook for about 20 minutes.
6. Take the cooker away from the heat and release pressure using the natural method.
7. Take the bay leaf out. Serve the dish while still hot, with grated cheddar cheese or sour cream for toppings; best enjoyed with homemade cornbread.

Lemoned Broccoli

One of the most popular vegetables, broccoli is often used as a side dish, and as ingredient in soups, salads, and different appetizers. Some people, however, prefer to keep things simple. Steamed broccoli on its own is a tasty and interesting side dish, but when eaten too often, it gets a bit boring. With this recipe, you will discover how adding an ingredient or two can make a huge difference!

Makes 4 to 6 servings

Preparation Time: 5 minutes

Cooking Time: 2 minutes

Ingredients:

- 900 grams of broccoli
- 125 ml water
- 4 slices of lemon
- salt & pepper, to taste

Instructions:

1. Remove the broccoli stalks' tough parts.
2. Score the ends.
3. Put some water in the cooker.
4. Put the broccoli sprinkled w/ lemon juice.
5. As desired, season w/ salt & pepper.

6. Close and seal the pressure cooker.

7. Allow to cook for no more than 2 minutes at 15 psi.

8. Allow to cool down after cooking.

9. Serve on its own or with a main dish.

Additional Notes:

1. The dish is best served with meats and rice.

2. If desired, you can add some cooked red onions to the dish.

3. Only use fresh broccoli for this recipe.

Risotto with Artichoke Hearts

Risotto is traditionally an Italian rice dish, and is among the most frequently used method to prepare and eat rice in the country. This is just another one of the many versions.

Makes 4 servings
Preparation Time: 15 minutes
Cooking Time: 15 minutes

Ingredients:

- 175 g of chocolate graham cracker crumbs
- 2 x 240 g packages of cream cheese, softened
- 180 g Arborio rice
- 400 g artichoke hearts, chopped
- 25 g Parmesan cheese
- 250 ml chicken stock
- 250 ml water
- 40 ml white wine
- 2 garlic cloves, minced
- 1 1/2 tbsp fresh thyme
- 1 tbsp olive oil
- salt and pepper

Instructions:
1. At medium setting, heat the oil in the cooker.
2. Cook the rice for 2 minutes.
3. Put in the garlic and allow to cook for about a minute.
4. Get a bowl that fits properly in the pressure cooker. Mix the stock, wine, and garlic with the rice in the bowl. Cover the bowl with tinfoil.
5. Put some water in the pressure cooker.
6. Place the bowl on a steaming basket or cooking rack, and then put it inside the cooker.
7. Properly close and lock the pressure cooker lid, making sure that the regulator is placed properly o the vent pipe.
8. Allow to cook at 15 psi for about 8 minutes.
9. Once cooked, let the pressure naturally drop down.
10. Take the bowl out of the pressure cooker. Remove the tinfoil.
11. Put the cheese artichoke hearts, and thyme I the cooked dish.
12. Serve hot and enjoy!

Additional Notes:

1. Instead of fresh thyme, you can opt to use dry thyme, if desired.

2. Make a foil lifter if the bowl doesn't have handles or is difficult to remove from the cooker.

3. You can add other veggies you want in the risotto.

Vegetable Curry

You've probably done a variety of curry recipes before, but usually with meats like lamb, beef, and chicken, among others. This recipe will allow you to try a healthier version of the popular Indian dish – using various veggies.

Makes 6 servings

Preparation Time: 20 minutes

Cooking Time: 10 minutes

Ingredients:

- 3 potatoes
- 2 sweet potatoes
- 1 red onion
- 2 capsicums
- 275 g green peas
- 400 g of rinsed chickpeas
- 25 g chopped coriander
- 70 g chopped toasted almonds
- 90 ml of non-sweetened coconut milk
- 6 tbsps of mild curry paste
- 65 ml water

Instructions:

1. Heat some oil in the pressure cooker.
2. Put the onions in, and then sauté with salt & pepper for about 5 minutes.
3. Add the sweet potatoes, potatoes, curry paste, capsicum, water, and coconut milk.
4. Cover and lock the pressure cooker and allow it to reach the desired pressure.
5. Lower the heat to maintain the pressure. Allow to cook for 2 more minutes or until the veggies are all tender.
6. Release pressure using the quick release method. This is done by putting the cooker under running water with the lid on.
7. Once the pressure is released, carefully open the lead and then add the chickpeas and peas.
8. Garnish the dish with toasted almonds and coriander.
9. Serve and enjoy!

Additional Notes:

1. Vegetable is great with basmati rice.
2. If you prefer some meat in your curry, just sauté some skinless chicken thighs cut in chunks, and mix with the veggies.
3. You can adjust the spiciness of the dish by using a milder or hotter variety of curry paste.

Conclusion

I'd like to thank you and congratulate you for transiting my lines from start to finish.

I hope this book was able to help you prepare delicious and nutritious Crock Pot recipes for your family and learn the basics of pressure cooking, as well as important tips on how to maximize the use of your pressure cooker.

The next step is to plan your meals ahead and start grocery shopping for the ingredients that you need. Also apply everything that you learned from this book and start whipping healthy and tasty pressure cooked meals that the whole family will enjoy.

I wish you the best of luck!

John Web

17629187R00082

Printed in Great Britain
by Amazon